LAUGH-OUT-LOUD JOKES

LAUGH-OUT-LOUD GROSS JOKES

BY LEONA FOWLER

WINDMILL BOOKS

Published in 2026 by Windmill Books, an Imprint of Rosen Publishing
2544 Clinton St., Buffalo, NY 14224

First Edition

Editor: Caitie McAneney
Book Design: Claire Zimmermann

Photo Credits: Cover, p.1 (child) aleks333/Shutterstock.com; series art (paper texture) OanaGherghe2/Shutterstock.com; series art (illustrations throughout) Look_Studio/Shutterstock.com; series art (illustrations) cover, p.1 (cockroach, poop), pp. 8, 18, 20 Nadzin/Shutterstock.com; p. 5 menur/Shutterstock.com; p. 7 Bildagentur Zoonar GmbH/Shutterstock.com; p. 9 Igor Meghega/Shutterstock.com; p. 11 aleks333/Shutterstock.com; p. 13 patpitchaya/Shutterstock.com; p. 15 maxim ibragimov/Shutterstock.com; p. 17 W. Scott McGill/Shutterstock.com; p. 19 Vladimir Bolokh/Shutterstock.com; p. 21 Paul.vsky/Shutterstock.com.

Library of Congress Cataloging-in-Publication Data

Names: Fowler, Leona, author.
Title: Laugh-out-loud gross jokes / Leona Fowler.
Description: Buffalo : Windmill Books, 2026. | Series: Laugh-out-loud jokes | Includes index.
Identifiers: LCCN 2025006418 (print) | LCCN 2025006419 (ebook) | ISBN 9781538399118 (library binding) | ISBN 9781538399101 (paperback) | ISBN 9781538399125 (ebook)
Subjects: LCSH: Wit and humor, Juvenile.
Classification: LCC PN6166 .F69 2026 (print) | LCC PN6166 (ebook) | DDC 818.6/02-dc23/eng/20250224
LC record available at https://lccn.loc.gov/2025006418
LC ebook record available at https://lccn.loc.gov/2025006419

Manufactured in the United States of America

CPSIA Compliance Information: Batch #CSWM26. For further information, contact Rosen Publishing at 1-800-237-9932

CONTENTS

Words in the glossary appear in **bold** the first time they are used in the text.

TOILET TALK

What did one toilet say to another?

"ARE YOU OKAY? YOU LOOK FLUSHED."

Which fairy hangs out in a bathroom?

STINKERBELL.

Why were there candles in the bathroom?

FOR THE BIRTHDAY POTTY.

Why did the superhero always flush the toilet?

BECAUSE IT WAS HIS DOODY!

FUN FACT!

The first flush toilet was **designed** for Queen Elizabeth I in 1596.

MAKING A STINK

How do you keep a skunk from smelling?

JUST HOLD ITS NOSE!

What happens if you eat too much alphabet soup?

YOU HAVE A HUGE VOWEL MOVEMENT.

Why are ninja toots dangerous?

THEY'RE SILENT, BUT DEADLY.

What are the two smelliest letters in the English language?

P. U.

FUN FACT!

A skunk's spray, called musk, can be smelled up to 1.5 miles (2.4 km) away!

TRICKY JOKES

What's brown and sticky?

A STICK—WHAT ELSE DID YOU THINK?!

Why don't people like poop jokes?

BECAUSE THEY STINK!

Knock knock.

WHO'S THERE? Europe.

EUROPE WHO?

No, YOU'RE a poo!

Toilets are good for two reasons.

NUMBER ONE AND NUMBER TWO.

FUN FACT!

Poop's smell comes from the **bacteria** in the **colon** that helps break food down.

PASS IT ON

What's a king's fart called?

A NOBLE GAS.

What happens when a clown passes gas?

THEY SMELL FUNNY.

What did the poop say to the toot?

"YOU BLEW ME AWAY!"

Why don't skeletons pass gas in public?

THEY DON'T HAVE THE GUTS!

FUN FACT!

"Farting" is the body's way of getting rid of extra gas that builds up due to swallowed air from eating or drinking, as well as **digestion.**

BOOGER BITS

What monster can you find on the end of your finger?

THE BOOGEYMAN!

What's the difference between boogers and vegetables?

KIDS DON'T EAT THEIR VEGETABLES!

What did the kid yell at the booger?

"YOU THINK YOU'RE FUNNY, BUT YOU'RE SNOT!"

How much do boogers weigh?

SNOT MUCH.

FUN FACT!

Boogers can be all different colors! Clear **mucus** is healthy, while yellow or green may mean you're sick.

THE NOSE KNOWS

How do you keep your nose from running?

STEAL ITS SHOES!

Did you pick your nose?

NOPE, I WAS BORN WITH IT!

What did the finger say to the nose?

"I'M SO GLAD I PICKED YOU."

Why was the nose sad?

IT WAS TIRED OF BEING PICKED ON.

FUN FACT!

The nose and throat make about a quart of mucus a day! Some stays in the nose, while most of it is swallowed.

GROSS JOBS

Why wouldn't the teacher pass gas in public?

HE WAS A PRIVATE TOOTER.

What did the paleontologist say when he found a **fossil** fart?

"IT'S A BLAST FROM THE PAST!"

Why did the baker's hands smell?

HE KNEADED A POO!

What do you call a booger in space?

AN ASTROSNOT!

FUN FACT!

Paleontologists may not find fossilized farts, but they do find fossilized poop. It's called a coprolite.

DISGUSTING DINOS

Why are pterodactyls so quiet in the bathroom?

THEIR "P" IS SILENT.

What game does a T-rex like to play with humans?

SQUASH.

What does a triceratops sit on?

ITS TRICERA-BOTTOM.

What do you call a dinosaur who won't take a shower?

A STINK-O-SAURUS.

FUN FACT!

Pterodactyls included several kinds of winged reptiles that died out around 66 million years ago.

CREATURE FEATURES

What did the cow poop say to the flies?

"DINNER'S ON ME!"

What's a cow without legs?

GROUND BEEF.

Where do sheep pee?

IN THE BAAAA-THROOM.

Why do ducks have feathers on their behinds?

TO COVER THEIR QUACKS.

FUN FACT!

Ducks pop their heads underwater to feed on plants and critters below the water's surface.

GLOSSARY

bacteria: Tiny, single-celled organisms. Some cause diseases in humans.

colon: Part of the large intestine.

design: To make the plans for something.

digestion: The process by which food is broken down into simpler forms to be used by the body.

fossilized: Having been turned into a fossil, or a trace of an organism from long ago.

knead: To form and shape something with the hands, especially dough.

mucus: A thick, sticky fluid that helps trap dust and other particles.

noble gas: A group of gases that are very stable, such as helium, neon, and argon.

vowel: In English, the letters a, e, i, o, and u.

FOR MORE INFORMATION

BOOKS

McAneney, Caitie. *Fun with Puns.* Buffalo, NY: Windmill Books, 2025.

Mason, Paul. *The Farts That Animals Blart.* Buffalo, NY: Gareth Stevens, 2026.

WEBSITES

10 Facts About Poop Everyone Should Know
humanbodylearning.com/fun-facts-about-poop-kids/
Learn the science behind poop and why it's so important for your body!

Your Digestive System
kidshealth.org/en/kids/digestive-system.html
Explore the digestive system, the body system that inspires so many jokes.

INDEX